Patchwork for Beginners

Patchwork for Beginners

By Sylvia Green

Watson-Guptill Publications, New York

First Printing, 1972

First published in the United States of America *1972* by Watson-Guptill Publications,
a division of Billboard Publications, Inc.,
165 West 46 Street, New York, N.Y.

Copyright © 1971 by Sylvia Green
First published in Great Britain by Studio Vista Limited in 1971
General editors Brenda Herbert and Janey O'Riordan

Manufactured in the U.S.A.

Library of Congress Cataloging in Publication Data

Green, Sylvia, 1915-
  Patchwork for beginners.
  Bibliography: p.
   1. Patchwork. I. Title.
TT835.G74 1972   746.4'6   72-190514
ISBN 0-8230-3925-0

Contents

Fig. 1 Detail from a cushion cover by Ann Mary Pilcher. Hexagon patches, made from striped cotton, have been skilfully arranged with hexagons and lozenges, made from plain poplin, to produce this interesting mosaic pattern

Introduction

Patchwork is the traditional way of using up scraps of material left over from dressmaking and soft furnishing (upholstering). For generations the thrifty needlewoman has made a habit of saving her bits and pieces for future use, and magnificent patchwork quilts, treasured today as works of art, resulted from this natural and frugal instinct.

This fascinating craft, which is enjoying renewed popularity at the present time, will appeal to most people who enjoy plain sewing and working with lovely materials and colours. It is not difficult to learn, and requires little in the way of special equipment. It needs no special technical skill beyond the ability to prepare and fit the shapes together accurately, and to stitch neatly.

The character of all patchwork is determined by the materials used in its construction. It is the simple and direct way of working with the pieces which gives traditional patchwork its lively and unselfconscious charm. Today dress and furnishing fabrics are available in a greater variety of gay colours and prints, exciting new weaves, finishes and textures than ever before. Many of these lend themselves well to the traditional patchwork shapes. They offer the discerning and adventurous needlewoman the opportunity to express herself in a contemporary manner, while working in the same direct way as the creators of those patchwork quilts whose traditional design and ageless beauty we still enjoy and admire. It is the aim of this book to encourage her to do this.

It is generally assumed that patchwork is an excessively slow craft, involving a great expenditure of time and patience. In fact it can be one of the quickest and most simple ways of creating a colourful and decorative surface. Once begun, it becomes so absorbing, and grows so easily under the hand of the needlewoman, that it is difficult to put it down. Nevertheless, a patchwork quilt may seem too ambitious an undertaking, especially to the beginner. Smaller articles, such as cushion covers and chair pads, boxes, belts and bags can be quite as attractive and rewarding in their different ways. Evening stoles, made from silk pieces, can be rich and lovely; patchwork toys can be fun. All these smaller articles will provide the enthusiastic needlewoman with plenty of scope for learning about and enjoying this delightful craft, and for making things in patchwork which will be as much in character with the fashions and furnishings of today as was the traditional work in the home of two hundred and fifty years ago.

The early tradition in patchwork

The ability to introduce charm and colour as well as to provide necessary furnishings and comfort from very little is a great gift. By devizing and stitching quilts and coverlets of surpassing beauty, the industrious and thrifty needlewomen of the late eighteenth and early nineteenth centuries established patchwork as the household art which has become our rich inheritance. (It is interesting that patchwork was being made by women at a time when all other crafts were made exclusively by men.)

The principle of economy, which was the governing factor in this activity, extended beyond the collecting together of every precious fragment of 'flowered callicoe' or 'charming chints', to include time, and methods of working. Practical considerations were of primary importance — careful planning and contriving could save time and make the most effective use of the available materials. Short cuts in working were sought and taken whenever possible. It was not until the late nineteenth century, when women found themselves with time on their hands, and the craft was declining, that accomplishment came to be measured in terms of the number of small patches which went into a piece of work, without regard for time spent or fabric wasted in cutting.

One can only marvel at the artistry and ingenuity of the early patchworkers, and at the dauntless spirit in which they embarked upon their prodigious tasks. For in addition to large quilts or coverlets, the necessary furnishings for the four-poster bed (still in general use at that time) included curtains and vallances. That all these were made, together with smaller articles of furnishing such as chair covers and cushion squares, we may see from those examples which happily are still in existence.

The familiar association of the two words 'patchwork' and 'quilt' has given many people the impression that they are inseparable, but this is not so. Quilted bed furniture had long been in common use, but it happened that in the second half of the eighteenth century, when quilting was at the peak of its popularity and the new fashion for patchwork at its most flourishing, the ways of these two traditional crafts ran closely together. The patchwork quilt was valued for the wealth of colour and gaiety which it brought into the home, and from the end of the eighteenth century all the less wealthy households possessed a quilt (or quilts) with patterned patchwork on one side and the other side plain, except for the quilting stitches. Sometimes a patchwork quilt was made for 'best', to be handed down as an heirloom, and this was kept carefully wrapped and put away. This accounts for the well-preserved state of many examples.

The coverlet of applied work or patchwork had been made to lay on top of the quilt as a day cover, before it became popular practice to combine the two in the patchwork quilt. In the early nineteenth century, when cottons were cheap and plentiful, the patchwork coverlet regained favour and once more became fashionable.

The influence of the gaily coloured cotton 'chints', or 'painted callicoes' which were imported from India at the end of the seventeenth century can be seen in most of the eighteenth-century patchwork. When the importation of these popular and fashionable cottons was eventually restricted, every fragment from dressmaking became precious and was preserved for making furnishings of patchwork. The amount of material required to make one large coverlet or quilt would have been considerable, and white or unbleached calico, which was inexpensive and plentiful, was often used to augment the coloured prints. This called for disciplined and imaginative planning, and an appreciation of the value of plain unpatterned areas in a design, all of which is characteristic of most eighteenth and early nineteenth century work. A good example can be seen in figs 2 and 3.

Fig. 2 A beautiful French patchwork quilt of the 1850's. Richly-patterned borders made with squares and triangles, alternating with plain borders, are arranged arround a centre panel, and a border of printed cotton makes a charming edge to the quilt

Fig. 3 Detail from the patchwork quilt in fig. 2, showing how the patchwork shapes are repeated in the quilting

In the early coverlets and quilts one finds a great economy of shape. The most popular shapes were those which could easily be arrived at by methodical folding and cutting of the material — squares, triangles, rectangles and diamonds. It was not until about 1845, when patterns became more complicated, that templates became an accepted part of the patchworkers' equipment.

The character of patchwork is influenced by changing fashions more fundamentally than most other kinds of needlework. The fashion for dress prints in dark colours in the early nineteenth

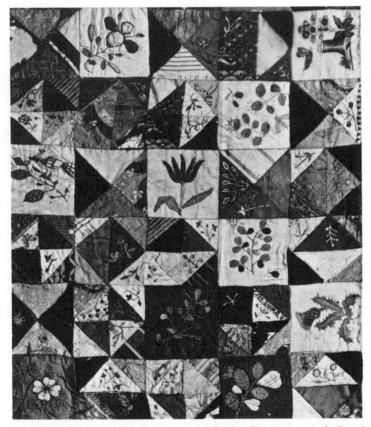

Fig. 4 Part of an eighteenth-century coverlet, English. The patchwork of silk and velvet is embroidered with silk, silver gilt and silver threads, with couched and applied work. This rich pattern of squares and triangles might inspire a design for a cushion in cotton fabrics, which would look delightful in a contemporary setting. Victoria and Albert Museum, London

century is recorded in the patchwork coverlets, just as the earlier fancy for the gaily coloured imported cottons had been. During the nineteenth century, silk and velvet became the popular dress materials, and these gradually replaced cotton and calico. Patchwork made with good quality silk and velvet has lasted well, but most silks were not strong enough to be used with velvet and comparatively little of this late nineteenth-century work remains in good condition today. The exceptionally beautiful eighteenth century coverlet (fig. 4) is remarkably well preserved, and shows how rich and lovely this combination can be.

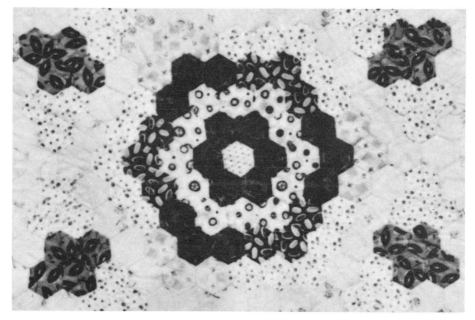

Fig. 5 This detail from the coverlet in fig. 6 shows how the elaborate pattern of the centre panel has been built up around the arrangement of hexagons known as the Rosette (see page 38). Victoria and Albert Museum, London

Fig. 6 Part of a coverlet made about 1837, English. Patchwork of printed cotton hexagons. Victoria and Albert Museum, London

The present-day needlewoman has a fine tradition on which to build, and plenty of good and inexpensive materials, especially cottons, with which to create patchwork which is contemporary in character and expressive of the tastes and fashions of this age. There is evidence of an awareness among young designers of the possible potentialities of both patchwork and quilting for practical and interpretative purposes, and that a very thorough exploration is being made in the light of new thought.

Fig. 7 A nineteenth-century quilt made in the USA. Patchwork of printed cotton in the Star of Bethlehem pattern, which grows from a simple arrangement of eight diamonds (see page 44). Victoria and Albert Museum, London

Fabrics

Patchwork is a way of making odd pieces of material, which might not otherwise be used, into something gay and useful. This is part of its charm and fascination, and it is the discrimination and ingenuity with which these pieces are selected and used which creates its lively and colourful character.

The need to choose carefully the best materials for making patchwork, from the bewildering number of natural and man-made fabrics at our disposal today, is not always appreciated. The lasting quality of your patchwork will depend, in the first instance, on the material from which the individual patches are made. It is a mistake to assume that, in the interests of economy, any available materials may be used; for it is obvious that some will be better than others. Patchwork demands precision and accuracy in the making, and fabrics which have a firm, even weave, which will crease and seam well, and will not fray, are the most suitable and the easiest to work with. Tradition has shown that cotton and linen fabrics lend themselves well to the shapes and patterns, and have been found to be practical and hardwearing.

Cotton, perhaps, has shaped the craft of patchwork to a greater extent than any other fabric. It is ideal in weave and texture, worthy of fine needlework, and easily laundered. More cotton patchwork has survived from the past than any other kind. Cottons are in good supply today and are among the most beautiful and popular materials in use for dress and furnishing purposes. They are made in a great variety of surfaces, weaves, colours and finishes, and most are excellent. Among them, the glazed or semi-glazed cottons, whether dress or furnishing weight, are the best and most pleasant to work with. They have all the necessary qualities to aid precision in making the shapes, and to give a crisp, even finish to your needlework. In common with most cottons, they are made in fast colours and in prints of good design, suitable for patchwork. Striped pillow ticking has the same qualities and can be used in a number of simple and effective ways. Other cottons which have proved their worth are poplin (fig. 30), piqué, sateen (fig. 48), and corduroy velvet (figs 10, 93). Good quality cotton mixtures may be used, and Viyella, which is a light-weight wool and cotton mixture, is made in many lovely colours and designs which will provide inspiration as well as appropriate pieces.

Calico, bleached and unbleached, has an unbroken tradition of

Fig. 8 Alms bag by Beryl Dean. Patchwork of silk and lurex fabrics in reds and golds, black and ivory, makes this rich pattern of squares and triangles

Fig. 9 Detail from a patchwork panel by Ann Mary Pilcher

use for every process in the making of patchwork, whether as a background for applied work, as pieced with cotton prints, or as a lining. It is made in a number of different widths and weights, and is easy and pleasant to handle and work with. Its value as a material of sufficient quality to be successfully pieced and sewn into patterns with other cottons might profitably be more widely recognized and rediscovered today.

Linen has as many excellent qualities as cotton, and is made in good fast colours and a variety of weights. The finer linens are easy to use, and lend themselves to all shapes and patterns. The coarser linens require more care in the making up, and it may be necessary to avoid using those shapes with points, such as the long diamond.

Experience of working with fabrics will quickly develop the ability to discriminate and to select those best suited to the size and the shape of the templates, and the purpose of the finished article. It cannot be stressed too often that good quality materials — capable of withstanding wear, and washing or dry cleaning, and worthy of the needlework entailed in the making — are essential. It is a waste of time and labour to work with poor quality or unsuitable materials. All those already mentioned are natural fabrics, sympathetic to the craft and pleasant to work with; they are safe, reliable, and, unless mishandled, bound to give satisfactory results.

Rayons and other man-made fabrics cannot be recommended unreservedly. Rayon is made in a variety of surfaces and finishes, some of which may appear temptingly rich and attractive, but most are difficult to control and will fray badly when cut. Many will stretch. A rayon and cotton mixture may possibly be used with success, and is certainly very strong. The safest way will be to look for the three essential qualities — if it will crease and seam well, if it has a firm texture, and will not fray when cut — then, providing the weight is right for the size of the templates and the purpose of the article, it may be used. Otherwise it should be rejected. Most materials which are entirely synthetic are not suitable for patchwork.

Pure silk of fine quality will make beautiful patchwork. It needs a little extra care in the handling and making up, and it may be an advantage to cut the shapes from a slightly stiffer paper or cardboard; this will help to ensure a crisp, flat finish to your work. As it will not stand up to daily wear and tear as successfully as cotton and linen, it is more suitable for rather precious things — for example an evening stole, a jewel box, a cushion cover for a special place, a tea cosy for special occasions.

Velvet, too, is rich and lovely; and in the hands of a skilled and experienced needlewoman can be used satisfactorily for certain purposes. It is not recommended to the inexperienced worker, for it has a particular characteristic which makes it difficult to manage. This is its habit of 'creeping', or moving in a contrary manner, which creates difficulty in covering the paper patterns and preparing the shapes for stitching, as a very little experimenting will reveal. The direction of the pile must be considered too, and care taken to ensure that the fabric is not permanently marked by pinning or tacking. It will be necessary to cut the pattern shapes from stiffer paper or card than when working with smoother and more amenable fabrics. Velvet is strong and will stand up to a good deal of wear if it is properly used and cared for. Like silk, it is suitable for more special things and purposes, and smaller things — such as an evening bag, a luxurious belt, or a cushion. It should be remembered that the weight of velvet, unlike silk, is considerable. This can present problems for the single-handed worker who undertakes a large piece of work. Generally speaking, it is not a good idea to piece velvet and silk together, as was the popular practice in the middle of the last century. Not only will the difference in the thickness of the two materials make it difficult to fit the geometric shapes together accurately and flatly, but the pile of the velvet will need careful brushing to keep it free from dust; this will pull the more fragile silk, and in time, cause it to tear and fray. In the case of those articles which are not subject to constant use (or which are disposable, such as balls) this may not matter, but for most practical purposes, velvet and silk are better used separately. However, if care is taken to match the weight, some lurex materials can be used to wonderful effect with either silk or velvet (see fig. 70).

Woollen fabrics and tweeds are made in a wide range of weights, textures, weaves and colours nowadays; and it is worth taking time and trouble to experiment with some to discover those which lend themselves well to the geometric shapes, and are pleasant and easy to work with. Many of them can be used to create patchwork of real character and individuality. The cushion in fig. 10 has been pieced with woollen fabrics and corduroy velvet in strongly contrasting tones, to give a bold pattern, and rich textural interest; and the beautifully made handbag in fig. 11 shows a very skillful and discerning use of tweed pieces.

Experiments can be made with every kind of material, once you are knowledgeable and experienced in your craft. In this way you will discover how effectively contemporary fabrics can be used

Fig. 10 Cushion by Christine Hawkins. Woollen furnishing (upholstery) fabrics and corduroy velvet in well contrasted tones make this bold mosaic pattern

with the traditional shapes to create work in a modern idiom. If you are a beginner, however, it would be as well to learn your craft with materials which are trusty and well tried, such as cotton. Then you will be able to embark on work with more unusual and exotic materials with confidence, and greater assurance of success.

Fig. 11 This unusual handbag by J. I. Burgess is pieced with woollen tweed fabrics. The skillful making up, and the considered and appropriate finish, enhance the excellence of the design and the needlework. A hand-made knotted cord makes the handle

Tools and equipment

A large part of the attraction of patchwork lies in its economical nature, and in the fact that most of the things which are needed for its making can so easily be found in the home. Templates are an essential part of the patchworker's equipment. Otherwise the usual contents of a workbox — scissors, thimble, pins, needles. tacking (basting) and sewing cotton — together with a selection of pieces of material, and paper from which to cut the pattern shapes, is all that is required.

Templates

The templates are the very accurate master shapes by means of which the paper patterns, over which each patch is constructed, are cut. They are usually made of metal or a hard plastic, and are produced commercially today in most of the traditional geometric shapes, and in a variety of sizes (for suppliers see page 102). The price list will show a pair of templates for each given size and shape, a 'solid' and a 'window' (see fig. 12). The solid represents the size of the finished patch, and is the pattern from which the paper linings are cut; the window is for selecting and marking out the actual patches on the fabric. Templates can be made at home from stiff cardboard (for temporary use), or zinc, both of which can be cut with strong scissors, or from copper or Perspex if the proper tools are available. However they are made, they must be extremely accurate, and skill and great care are required in the cutting. It may be possible for the amateur to cut large shapes satisfactorily, but it is probably better and safer to buy the smaller shapes ready-made.

Paper

The paper for the linings over which each patch is constructed needs to be firm enough to allow the fabric to crease over the edges crisply, and sufficiently flexible to fold with the material as the patchwork progresses. A good quality writing paper is suitable, also the backs of old greeting cards, the pages of company directors' annual reports, and other papers of similar quality. It is part of the economy of patchwork that paper should not be bought specially for this purpose!

Scissors

Two pairs of good scissors will be needed — one pair for cutting the paper patterns, and the other for cutting the fabric patches. These should be fairly small, very sharp, and pointed. If you prefer to cut the papers with a craft (mat) knife, you will need a flat metal plate or similar hard surface for cutting on.

Pins

Pins should always be fine and smooth, in order to minimize the risk of marking the fabrics. Brass lace pins are suitable for all purposes, and are the best. Steel dressmakers' pins can be used satisfactorily for heavier materials, and the very short fine pins known as 'lills' or 'lillikins' are just right for small patches.

Needles

Needles should be as fine as the material and your eyesight will allow, and sizes 9 and 10 are most generally useful. In any case, do not try to work with a needle which is coarser than size 7. Fine needles and thread will aid the close stitching which is required to make strong, neat seams. Either Sharps or Betweens may be used, according to preference; some people find the shorter Betweens easier and more pleasant to work with.

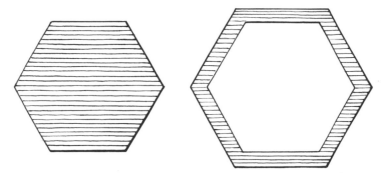

Fig. 12 A pair of templates: left, solid; right, window

Thread

Cotton thread is suitable for most fabrics, with the exception of fine silk, which should be sewn with a silk thread. Heavy silk is better sewn with cotton. Linen, velvet, and satin may also be sewn with a cotton thread. The cotton should be fine, as stitches will be small and close; numbers 60, 80, or 100 will suit most fabrics. As a general rule use white cotton for all light coloured patches, and black cotton for all dark patches. When joining a light and a dark patch, a dark thread will show the stitches less than a light one.

Thimble

A thimble will help you to work more rhythmically and quickly; it will also prevent sore fingers.

Additional items

Occasionally it may be necessary to do some unpicking. A sharp razor blade, or a seam ripper, will do this more easily and effectively than a pair of scissors.

A sharp pencil may be used for marking out the position of the patches on the wrong side of the fabric. This ensures that the material is not cut wrongly or wastefully. If the shapes must be marked on the right side, because the pattern does not show clearly on the wrong, or if the material is dark, a white dressmakers' pencil should be used. Never use a ballpoint pen on fabric.

It is an advantage to have a flat surface on which to plan patterns with the prepared patches. For working on your knees, a cork bath mat, or a flat board with a similarly soft surface, is ideal. The patches can be pinned in position when you have decided on the arrangement, and left in place when the work has to be put aside.

Fig. 13 Patchwork box by Ann Mary Pilcher

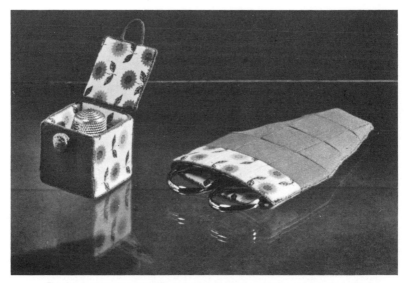

Fig. 14 A charming scissors case and thimble·container made by Doris Cook

Patchwork — the craft

By selecting the most suitable fabrics and equipping yourself with the proper tools in the first place, you will be making provision for achieving more easily the qualities of precision and accuracy which are essential to the making of pieced patchwork. The good craftsman is one who knows and respects his materials, and understands how to use them effectively, with skill and dexterity. It is through experience and practice in working with them, and to some extent by trial and error, that this knowledge and ability is acquired. The following suggestions are made to help you to make a good start.

The choice of template

The equilateral hexagon, or Honeycomb, is the easiest shape to construct and piece accurately, and is recommended to the beginner. The size of the template for your first exercises should be not less than one inch (this being the measurement of each edge of the six-sided shape). The hexagon can be arranged in a variety of ways to create rich mosaic patterns and gay borders. Besides helping you to learn the essentials of the craft easily and enjoyably, it will provide plenty of scope for experimenting with tone and colour, pattern and texture.

The paper patterns

Cutting out the paper patterns is a very important part of patchwork, for these form the foundation for the construction of the whole fabric. A fractional inaccuracy in a paper will cause a misfit out of all proportion to its apparent insignificance, when the patches are sewn together. All the patterns for one piece of work should be cut from paper of a uniform thickness. If they are cut from papers of different thickness, the patches will not be identical and this will spoil the precision of the patchwork.

Using the solid template as guide, the patterns are cut out directly with scissors, the blades hugging the edge of the hard shape and making one sharp cut on each of the six sides (see fig. 15). After a little practice in holding the paper and the template firmly together, the cutting can be done easily and accurately. By folding the paper the patterns may be cut out two at a time, but it is not advisable to attempt to cut from more than two thicknesses. On no account should the patterns be made by drawing round the template with a pencil line and cutting out from this. It is almost impossible to cut accurate patterns in this way. When the work is complete, the paper patterns will be removed, and if this is done carefully there is no reason why they should not be used again.

Although the instructions given here and in the following paragraphs apply specifically to the hexagon, the procedure is the same for all the geometric shapes.

The choice of fabric

A good quality cotton material is the obvious choice for the beginner, whether for practice work or for the first patchwork article. Do not make the mistake of thinking that 'anything will do' for your first exercises. The selected pieces should be of new, unused material. This will help you to achieve the firm, crisp finish which is so desirable, and to set yourself a high standard from the beginning. All the patches for one piece of work should be cut from fabric of a similar weight and thickness, otherwise the geometric shapes will not fit together exactly, and the finished work will not lie flat.

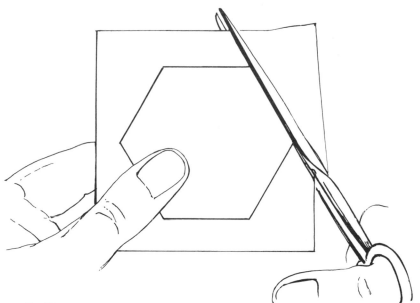

Fig. 15

Cutting out the patches

The success and durability of your patchwork will depend upon the proper use and cutting of the material. In cutting out patches of any shape, there are two main considerations. The first is to make the best use of the printed or woven pattern to construct the design of the patchwork, the second is that whenever possible the patches should be cut in accordance with the warp of the fabric.

The window template (fig. 16) conveniently shows the effect of the finished patch, and will assist you in selecting the required area of fabric and in planning the design. It makes adequate allowance for turnings, and can be used to cut the patches directly, by holding the template firmly to the right side of the fabric and cutting out round the shape. Alternatively, if you are an inexperienced worker, you may prefer to do it in the following way: place the fabric on a flat surface, wrong side up; hold the template firmly in place and draw round the shape with a finely pointed HB pencil (or a white dressmakers' pencil if the material is dark)

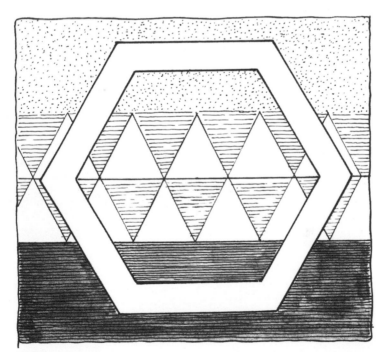

Fig. 16

and then cut out the patch. This method has the advantage of enabling you to detect and correct any errors without spoiling the fabric.

It is a sound principle that when cutting out the patches, the thread of the fabric should run the same way in as many patches as possible. Clearly, the way in which you use the pattern of the fabric to make the design, or the size and shape of a precious scrap of exactly the right colour, may preclude your following this rule in every instance. But it is particularly desirable to follow it when patches of the same material and colour are to be stitched together to form a background area, and it will contribute immeasurably to the look and good wearing quality of the finished work, especially in the case of a washable article.

In cutting hexagon patches (or those of similar shape, such as the octagon) in accordance with the weave of the fabric, two sides of the template should lie at right angles to the warp, or alternatively they should be placed parallel with it (see fig. 17).

Fig. 17

Making the patches

The tacking together (basting) of the fabric and the paper patterns is the final stage in the preparation of the patches for stitching, and it is the most time consuming process in the making of pieced patchwork. It requires the utmost precision, for together with the careful and correct cutting of the papers and the fabric, it is the foundation of accurate construction.

The diagrams show, step by step, how to make a hexagon patch (instructions for making other shapes are given in the relevant sections).

A paper pattern is placed in the centre of the patch on the wrong side of the fabric (fig. 18). The patch is more easily handled if the paper is pinned in position at this stage, but before doing so you should make sure that the surface of the fabric will not be permanently marked by the pin pricks. Glazed cotton, silk and satin are especially liable to be damaged by this, and should not be pinned; most unglazed cottons will not suffer.

The patch is held with the paper pattern uppermost. The hem of the fabric is folded crisply over each side, and tacked to the paper. It is usually sufficient to take one stitch into each side, allowing the thread to cross the corners and secure the hem (fig. 20). Finish by taking an extra stitch into the first side, and cut the thread to leave about one quarter of an inch. In tacking (basting), the

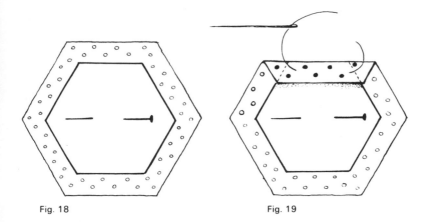

Fig. 18   Fig. 19

thread should be drawn to a firm, even tension. It should never be secured by means of a knot or a back stitch, for this would impede the removal of the tacking stitches when the work is complete, and might pull the fabric.

The proper handling of the fabric is important at this stage. Some fabrics (and shapes) are more amenable than others, and some need more careful treatment than others. Your skill and knowledge will grow through practice in working. In particular, care should be taken that the surface of a fabric is not marked by pinning or tacking (basting). Stitches should never be taken through the paper to the right side of the patch when working with any delicate or easily marked fabric (glazed cotton, silk or satin, for example). If the fabric is one which is not easily marked, it may be harmless, and convenient on occasions, to stitch through to the right side of the patch. At all times every care should be taken to avoid spoiling the freshness of the material.

In making a patch from velvet, the problem created by the movement of the fabric known as 'creeping' may be met by cutting more generous turnings than those allowed for by the window template. While the pile of the velvet may successfully cover marks made by pins, it can be permanently marked by a tacking stitch being drawn too tight.

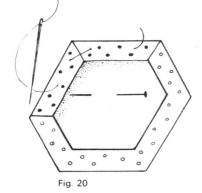

Fig. 20

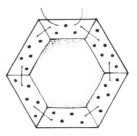

Fig. 21

Joining the patches

The patches are joined by seaming or over-sewing on the wrong side, with small even stitches. In learning how to join hexagons you will need three prepared patches. Hold the first two patches with the right sides face to face, and the papers outwards. Make sure that the two edges to be seamed are matched exactly, and that the stitching begins and finishes precisely at either end of the seam. Any gaps in the stitching will show on the right side and will spoil and weaken your patchwork. The thread is sewn in for about a quarter of an inch before you begin seaming, so that knots may be avoided, and finished off by sewing back for a few stitches before cutting. Sew with neat, fine stitches and a firm (but not tight) tension, taking up with the needle a thread or two only from the edge of each patch, and avoiding the paper. The stitches should be fairly close, but not so close that the fabric is pulled or split, or that the joined patches are unable to lie flat. You will find that sixteen stitches to one inch is about right for most fabrics. When the two patches are joined, open the seam and press flat, on the wrong side. The stitches will not be entirely invisible on the right side, but if they are fine and even this will not matter.

The third patch fits into place as shown in fig. 22. Match the two edges exactly as before, and begin to stitch at A. The angle at B must fit very accurately, and be stitched meticulously. Then seam with the same thread from B to C. By seaming together three patches like this, you will learn everything about joining hexagons.

In constructing any large area of patchwork, such as the bed-cover in fig. 31, it is usually easier to join the patches in convenient groups or units (as the design allows or dictates), and subsequently to sew these together to complete the finished article. With a little forethought it will be possible to arrange that several patches are seamed with the same thread, which is an advantage. However, the length of your working thread should not exceed eighteen inches. Fine threads tend to knot easily, if sewn against the twist. The thread should always be cut, not broken, and the end which comes first off the reel should be threaded in the needle. If the thread is cut across at an angle it will thread more easily into a fine needle.

Where the design of the patchwork allows, it is sound practice in joining the patches (as in cutting out), to arrange that the thread of the fabric runs the same way in as many as possible, especially those making background areas. This will help to avoid creases and puckers and to give crispness and precision to your work.

Information about joining shapes other than the hexagon are given in the relevant sections, where necessary.

Removing the papers

The paper patterns may remain in place until the patchwork is complete; this will help to keep it fresh and crisp. Before removing tackings (basting stitches) and papers it is beneficial to press the work on the wrong side lightly, unless the fabric is so delicate that it is likely to be marked on the surface by the tacking stitches, or if it is material with a pile, such as velvet.

To remove the papers, lay the work on a flat surface, snip the thread once on each patch, and withdraw the tackings (basting stitches) carefully, so that the fabric is not pulled. The papers may be lifted out. It is now that you will appreciate the absence of knots and backstitches!

Most patchwork articles will require lining and appropriate finishing. For more about this, see page 96.

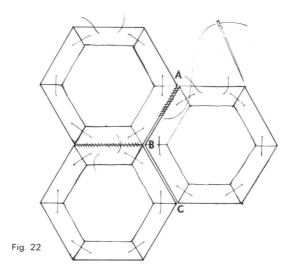

Fig. 22

The satisfaction you will find in the accurate working and smooth finish of your sewn patchwork will be ample reward for the time and care spent on the initial selection and preparation of the patches.

The 'bit bag' or 'piece box' is an essential part of every needle-woman's equipment, and it provides the main source of supply for the patchworker. These pieces, purposefully hoarded for future use, will often provide inspiration as well as patches; and, as you gain experience in working with fabrics and shapes, your eye will be quick to recognize those printed designs which lend themselves well to your patchwork patterns.

As a general rule, patches should be made from new, unused fabric. Pieces saved from the good parts of used materials — such as little-worn areas from clothing and furnishings — may be suitable if they are still fresh and unfaded, but they should be well tested. If patches of new fabric are to be sewn with them, in the same piece of work, the new fabric should be washed before use. This will lessen the risk of work being spoiled by shrinking after the first wash.

It is contrary to the nature of patchwork to buy all the material for a piece of work, but it may sometimes happen that your 'patchwork eye' will detect exciting possibilities in a printed design, and you will buy half a yard with some specific plan in mind. This may be a fruitful and interesting way of working on occasion; it can produce new ideas, as well as a new look for patchwork. The cushions in figs 72–3, illustrate this approach, and show how successful it can be.

However, it is the contriving and ingenuity with which the available pieces are used which has always given to patchwork its particular richness and character, and which is the essence of its multi-coloured charm. This fact should not be overlooked, especially as there is all the delight of the unexpected in this way of planning and working. It may be necessary to buy some extra pieces, especially if a considerable amount of one colour is used for a background, or when a design needs a touch of a special colour to give it life, but this is legimate.

Finally, in selecting your pieces remember that the success of your patchwork will depend upon the quality of every single patch. For all practical purposes, do not use different kinds of fabric in one piece of work; one may wash and wear better than another.

Always be careful to select and use pieces of similar weight and thickness, otherwise the shapes will not fit accurately and the thinner fabric will tear away from the thicker. For some very special purposes, rich fabrics such as silk, velvet, or Lurex may be used together with beautiful effect in the same piece of work (see figs 44, 70), but this demands considerable technical accomplishment, knowledge of fabrics, and experience in working with them. Smaller and more ephemeral articles — such as belts, balls, toys and pincushions — will provide opportunities for the beginner to experiment with a variety of fabrics before attempting anything on a more ambitious scale.

Fig. 23 Patchwork of plain and printed cotton is used in this delightful design which is based on a simple arrangement of hexagon rosettes

Fig. 24 Pincushion by Patricia Horne. An ingenious arrangement of printed cotton hexagons makes this charming design

Fig. 25 The other side of the pincushion showing an equally attractive use of fabric and shapes

Geometric shapes and patterns

Patterns built up from geometric shapes are to be found in most crafts. In patchwork, the shapes are arranged in patterns and joined together to construct the whole fabric, just as mosaics and tiles are arranged to make decorative floors and walls. In other kinds of needlework — for example, embroidery, appliqué and quilting — they are used to give surface decoration. Quilting has a special affinity with patchwork, because some shapes are mutual to both — notably the square, the diamond and the shell. For this reason quilting and patchwork are often combined.

The earliest patchwork was made without the aid of templates and papers, and was probably pieced with squares or rectangles. The shapes were arrived at by folding, and cutting out directly with the thread of the fabric. From the diagrams on this page it can be seen how naturally diamonds, triangles, hexagons and octagons can be developed from these basic shapes.

The hexagon, the diamond, and the square have become the most popular shapes for patchwork. Each of these may be arranged and pieced in a variety of attractive ways, without the addition of any other shape, or they may be effectively combined with other shapes, to make patterns. The same is true of triangles and rectangles. The octagon is a good shape, but it must always be used with an additional shape to make a pattern, and the pentagon will not make up into flat patchwork without the addition of another shape.

There is no standard size for the shapes, they can be as large or as small as the patchwork article requires. Templates can be bought in a variety of sizes (for suppliers see page 102) or made at home to the size required. Diagrams showing the geometric construction of some of the shapes will be found in the following pages.

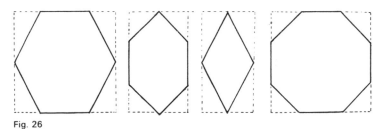

Fig. 26

The hexagon

The hexagon is the shape most characteristic of English patch-work. Three variations of this six-sided shape are found in the patterns.

The most popular is the equilateral hexagon, which makes the familiar honeycomb pattern. This is the easiest shape to construct and arrange in attractive patterns without other shapes, and the one which most successfully makes use of small oddments of material which might not combine so pleasingly in other ways. A beginner is well advised to explore the character and potentialities of one shape very thoroughly before moving on to others, and the hexagon is the ideal shape with which to begin, for it can be used to build such a variety of patterns.

The Rosette is the simplest and most fundamental arrangement. It is made with seven hexagons, six of them usually made from the same material, surrounding a centre one of contrasting colour or tone (see fig. 30). This motif can form the basis for countless patchwork patterns. The rosettes are usually made singly and joined together in strips or blocks, which in turn are seamed to complete the article. Single rosettes may be arranged in a pattern and applied onto a background of plain material; they can also be used in a variety of ways to make border patterns.

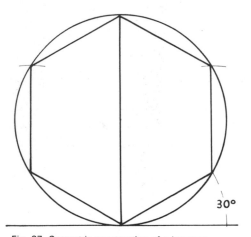

30°

Fig. 27 Geometric construction of a hexagon

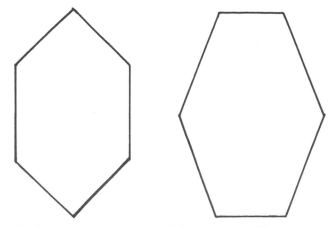

Fig. 28 Left, the long hexagon or Church window; right, the Coffin

Fig. 29 A useful and attractive display folder showing hexagon, Church Window
and Box patterns

Increasing the size of the single rosette with another ring of hexagons of a different colour will make the Double Rosette. A rich and beautiful use of this motif can be seen in fig. 31 opposite. Yet another ring, also different, will make the Treble Rosette, and so on. The illustration in fig. 6 shows an elaborate pattern developed from this very simple foundation.

The diamond motif (fig. 33) is made by adding two more hexagons to the single rosette. This too can be enlarged and developed in a variety of ways. It has, perhaps, greater distinction than the rosette and is more contemporary in character. It has been used successfully and skilfully by the maker of the quilt illustrated in fig. 32.

The long hexagon, or Church Window (fig. 28), is an attractive shape which combines well with squares and octagons to make patterns. It can also be used without additional shapes. The handbag in fig. 11 illustrates a very good use of the Church Window with the square.

The Coffin (fig. 28), the third variation of the hexagon shape, is seldom seen, perhaps on account of the associations with its name and shape. It is generally used alone.

Fig. 30 Tea cosy by W. M. Kendrew. Poplin, printed cotton, and gingham combine effectively to make this pattern, which is based on the Single Rosette. Notice particularly the way in which the hexagons have been used to join the two sides and to make a charming, neat edging

Fig. 31 Part of a patchwork bedcover by Elizabeth Cobb. Double Rosettes, made from a variety of Liberty lawn prints, make a gaily colourful pattern against the well contrasted plain dark cotton background

Fig. 32 Patchwork bedcover by Joan Bergh

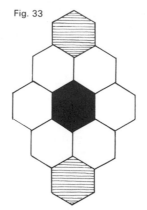

Fig. 33

This distinctive bedcover is made with $5/8$-inch hexagons. The carefully considered arrangement of the diamond units, allowing maximum value and richness on the white background, and the thoughtfully and imaginatively planned pattern of the whole, is all in the best patchwork tradition.

Fig. 34 Sampler from the display folder (fig. 29). The long hexagon or Church
Window, and the square (used diamond wise), combine to make this
all-over pattern. The plain dark cotton squares emphasize the pattern and
contrast well with the plain and printed cottons of the Church Window
shapes. These are made in reds and pinks, yellow and olive greens, and
have been carefully selected and arranged

The diamond

The diamond is more difficult to construct than the hexagon, because of the two pointed ends, but it is a popular shape which can be arranged to make a variety of attractive patterns. There are several variations of this shape, but the two most generally found are those based on the hexagon and the square. Of these, the diamond or lozenge, based on the hexagon, seems to be the more popular (fig. 35). The 'box' pattern is one of the best known arrangements of this shape (fig. 36), with the characteristic three-dimensional effect made by the dark, light, and medium tones of the three diamonds which are joined to make a hexagon. The 'box' has been used to make all-over and border patterns since the beginning of the nineteenth century; but, fascinating as it is, it can be over-insistent and disturbing on a flat surface, especially if the tonal contrast is too strong. Other arrangements of this diamond are the Six Pointed Star (fig. 42), the Zig-zag and the Trellis (figs 40, 41). It will also combine with the hexagon in a number of ways to make patterns. (figs 1, 64).

The diamond which is based on a square is usually known as the long diamond. It is the more difficult of the two to construct and piece, as the points are so sharply angled. This diamond can be arranged to make the eight pointed star, which is the basis of the Star of Bethlehem design (fig. 7). It seems to have been a particular favourite with American needlewomen, and many beautiful examples of this design are to be found in the patchwork quilts belonging to that country. In English patchwork, however, the long diamond is more often combined with squares and tri-angles.

The difficulty in constructing diamond patches comes in nego-tiating the double fold which the pointed ends necessitate, with-

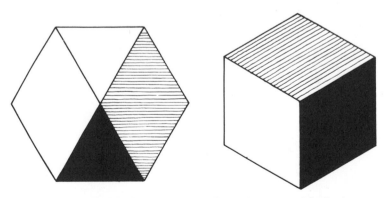

Fig. 35 Diamonds and half-diamonds made from a hexagon and the 'box'

Fig. 36 The 'box' pattern. Sampler from display folder (fig. 29). This example clearly illustrates the way in which three diamonds of light, medium and dark tones, can be joined to construct a hexagon and give the three-dimensional effect of a cube

out blunting them. The broad angles are exactly like the hexagon, and are folded in the same way. Evenly woven, firm-textured cottons and fine linens, which will fold and crease well, will help in achieving the precision and accuracy required in constructing and piecing this shape. Fabrics such as velvet, which 'creeps' and is too bulky, and rayons, which are slippery and will fray, should be avoided, but a good quality silk has the necessary attributes for successful use with the diamond.

In constructing the patches the procedure is the same as for the hexagon (see pp. 26–33). The pair of templates are used in the same way to prepare papers and patches. Paper or thin cardboard which is firm enough to resist the folding over of the fabric and give well pointed ends to the finished patch should be used for making the patterns. The patches should be cut out with regard to the warp of the material whenever possible. Two ways in which this may be done are shown in fig. 37. By placing the window template with two edges parallel with the warp (fig. 37A), the natural bias of this shape is limited to one direction, and the patch will be cut with the thread of the fabric on two sides. In the position fig. 37B, all four sides of the diamond will be cut on the bias and the warp thread will run vertically with the two points.

The diagrams (fig. 38) show, step by step, how to construct a diamond patch. It may be helpful to practise first with a patch cut from thin crisp paper, such as greaseproof. This will handle easily and show clearly the lines of each successive fold.

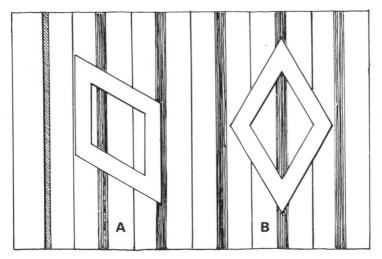

Fig. 37

PREPARING THE DIAMOND PATCH

1 Pin the paper pattern carefully in the centre of the patch.
2 Fold over and tack the right-hand hem first, A. Two tacking stitches are needed to keep the fabric firmly in place.
3 Fold over the fabric at the point as shown in B, so that the edge of the fold runs parallel with the edge of the paper pattern, but does not overlap it. Do not stitch this fold.
4 Fold over and tack the left-hand hem, taking a stitch into the folded corner, C.

Repeat the process for the remaining two sides of the diamond. Do not be discouraged if your first attempts are not successful, a little practice will soon make perfect.

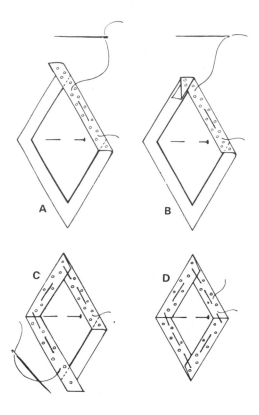

Fig. 38

The method of seaming diamond patches is the same as for the hexagon. So long as the edges of the shapes match well, it should be quite straightforward. Always stitch from the wide angled corner towards the pointed ends (fig. 39). It is especially important to remember to do this when diamonds are being joined to make a star pattern. The pointed ends should meet exactly in the centre, without leaving a hole, and the star should lie flat when pressed. This is not an easy thing to accomplish.

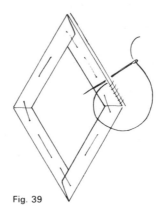

Fig. 39

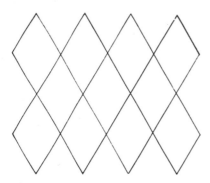

Fig. 40 The trellis

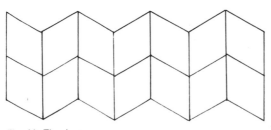

Fig. 41 The zig-zag

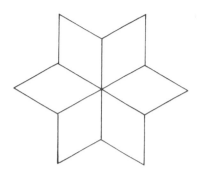

Fig. 42

Fig. 43 Spectacle case by Miriam
Moore. The case, and the
patchwork which is app-
lied, are made in a variety
of rich lurex fabrics. A
sequin is sewn into the
centre of each six-pointed
star

Fig. 44 This skilfully constructed patchwork pincushion by Miriam Moore is made up with sixty templates of thin card. The half-long-diamonds of lurex fabrics in golds, deep pinks and metallic blues, are stitched together in groups of three. Five hundred pins in all have been inserted along the joined edges, and a sequin is pinned at the apex of each pyramid to give a decorative finish

The half-diamond, or pyramid

Half-diamonds, or pyramids, based on the hexagon (fig. 35), or the long diamond, can be used to make border patterns, the most usual arrangement being the Dogs-tooth (hound's tooth) pattern. A good example of this can be seen in fig. 68. The half-diamond based on the hexagon will also combine with hexagons to make all-over patterns. An unusual use of the half long diamond is illustrated in fig. 44. When making half-diamond patches, fold the fabric over each of the three points in the same way as for the points of the diamond.

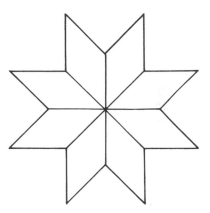

Fig. 45 The eight-pointed star, which is made with the long diamond

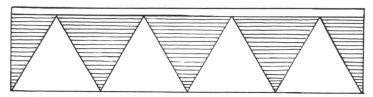

Fig. 46 The Dogs tooth (hound's tooth) pattern

Squares and triangles

The square is frequently found in early patchwork, and is almost as popular as the hexagon and the diamond. If it is used with imagination it can make attractive patchwork without the addition of other shapes, but it can easily give a monotonous effect. It will combine well with many other shapes. During the late eighteenth and early nineteenth centuries, when patches were made without the aid of templates, it was customary to vary the square by cutting the corners to make a diamond, and bisecting it diagonally to make triangles. Many of the finest designs of that period were pieced with this satisfying combination of shapes, and it is worthwhile making a careful study of some of these. A good example is shown in figs 2 and 3. Another arrangement of these simple shapes to give rich and varied pattern can be seen in figs 49 and 50. The square is more difficult than any other shape to construct accurately, and the slightest deviation from true will be apparent. It is usually easier for tacking (basting) to lay the patch on a flat surface, rather than holding it in the hand.

The triangle made by bisecting the square is the basis for a number of well known patchwork patterns, which are usually made in two colours only; among them the Windmill, the Cotton Reel, and the Basket (see page 55). These are particularly characteristic of American patchwork. It can also be arranged in a number of ways, without additional shapes, to make border patterns.

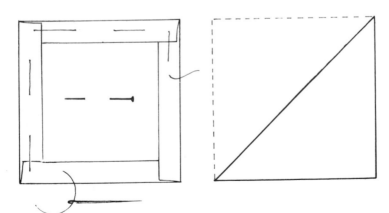

Fig. 47 The square and the triangle

Fig. 48 This lively lion by Jean McLeod is made with two-inch squares of cotton sateen. The foam filling is light and easy to handle. A simple foundational shape such as this is equally adaptable to a toy or a cushion for a child's room. Make some experiments for yourself

Fig. 49 Detail from an eighteenth-century coverlet showing a rich pattern of squares and triangles. Victoria and Albert Museum, London

Fig. 50 These shapes lend themselves particularly well to contemporary patch-work

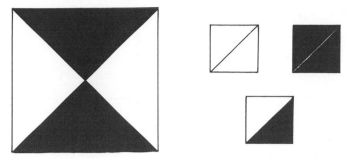

Fig. 51 The Cotton Reel. Identical squares of two contrasting colours are cut and arranged to make this pattern

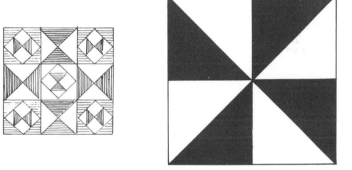

Fig. 52 The triangles are arranged differently to make the Windmill pattern

Fig. 53 This arrangement makes the popular Garden Basket pattern. This is usually pieced and applied to a background. The handle is also applied

The pentagon

The five-sided shape most often seen is the equilateral pentagon. Twelve equilateral pentagons automatically make up into a ball, but this shape will not make flat patchwork when stitched without other shapes. A more attractive five-sided shape is that which is made from a diamond with one point removed. This combines well with one hexagon and six diamonds to make a pattern called the Box and Star (see fig. 58), which readily lends itself to the making of pincushions and small boxes. Pincushions made in the same way as the ball, from a variety of precious scraps, can be very attractive too.

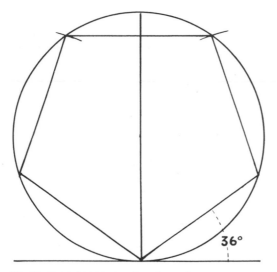

Fig. 54 Geometric construction of a pentagon

Fig. 55 Two pentagonal shapes

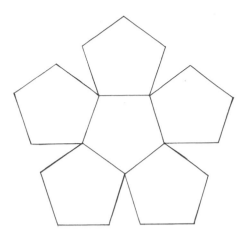

Fig. 56 Pentagons are stitched in two groups of six, which are then joined to make a ball

Fig. 57 A ball made by Ann Mary Pilcher in black and white felt pentagons, and embellished with applied felt shapes, simple embroidery stitches and sequins

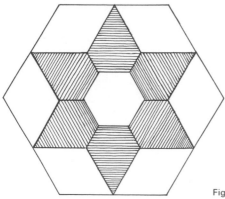

Fig. 58 The box and star pattern

Fig. 59 Six pentagonal shapes and a hexagon make this star-shaped pincushion
by Miriam Moore

The octagon

The eight-sided octagon has never been as popular as the hexagon, diamond and square. It is usually pieced with squares, and cannot be used without additional shapes. Long hexagons and triangles will also combine well with octagons. It is an easy shape to construct and piece, being similar to the hexagon, and it is less time consuming than some other shapes. Octagons look well in quite large sizes, and home-made templates can be cut without much difficulty. An exceedingly rich effect can be achieved by dividing a large octagon, as shown in the diagram in fig. 63, and piecing silk fabric, so that the light is caught at different angles. Octagons can also be arranged in groups to make pattern.

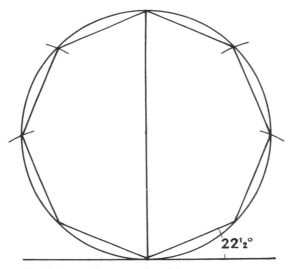

Fig. 60 Geometric construction of the octagon

Fig. 61 Cushion cover by Lesley Johnson of the Mary Boon School. Three and a half-inch octagons and squares make this pattern. Simple embroidery stitches enrich the large octagonal shapes. The difference in tone between the four dark red octagons and the other five, which are deep periwinkle blue, is less pronounced in the actual cushion cover

Fig. 62 Detail from the altar frontal designed by Joyce Conway Evans for King's College Chapel, Cambridge. The handwoven ground fabric is enriched with embroidery devized and created by Elisabeth Geddes assisted by Audrey Chaytor Morris, using couching, needleweaving, appliqué and various relief methods. The materials include gold and copper kid, and lurex fabrics. A study of this beautifully embellished pattern of octagons and squares may well inspire the enterprising patchworker

In the illustrations in this book you can see some of the ways in which the geometric shapes can be arranged and combined to make interesting and attractive patterns. You will enjoy discovering other ways for yourselves. Once you begin to 'see' in terms of this kind of pattern, you will find it appearing all around you — in tiled floor patterns, wrought iron, wood inlay, brickwork, for instance, as well as in examples of patchwork and quilting which you may see in homes or museums, or study from books (see page 102). It is very often the most simple arrangement of shapes (or of one single shape) which will make the most rich and satisfying patchwork pattern (see figs 2, 49 and 50), so do not try to do anything too ambitious or complicated. Economy in the use of shape (and in the use of time) is as fundamental to the craft of patchwork as is the thrifty and ingenious use of fabric.

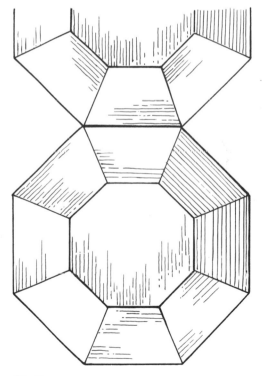

Fig. 63

Pattern design and colour

The final success of your patchwork will depend as much upon well planned design and a skilful use of colour as upon the accurate construction and piecing of the patches.

Patchwork makes its immediate appeal through the characteristic and lively qualities of colour and pattern. These two qualities are so mutually dependent that it is impossible to consider one without the other. The colour and the shape of the patches make an equal contribution to all good patchwork pattern. If the colour contrasts are not right, no satisfactory pattern will emerge. It is especially easy to appreciate this point when looking at a comparatively simple pattern such as the 'box', illustrated in fig. 36, which depends entirely on the arrangement of diamonds in three contrasting tones or colours for its characteristically three-dimensional effect.

The disciplined pattern made by the methodical assembling of the coloured patches is an essential element in all good patchwork design. A discerning choice of printed and coloured fabrics for making the patches is the first step towards achieving this. The relation and proportion of pattern to background (or pattern to plain) and to the size and shape of the article, are further important factors in the harmony of the final design.

Simple motifs, such as the 'box', the hexagon rosette and the six and eight-pointed star, form the basis of many patchwork patterns, and will provide a starting point from which to experiment with pattern and colour planning. The hexagon is the easiest shape to construct and piece, and the rosette motif, which is made by fitting one or more rings of hexagons round a centre patch, is the most popular and familiar arrangement of this shape. It is the ideal unit with which to begin exploring pattern design and colour.

Pattern and colour planning with the hexagon

Seven hexagons make a single rosette. Six of these are arranged in a ring around the centre patch. If the seven patches are assembled in a haphazard manner, without regard to the choice and arrangement of colour or print, the resulting shape will be indefinite, lop-sided or spotty. If, on the other hand, six hexagons of the same colour or print are carefully selected and pieced around a contrasting colour, both shape and pattern will be harmoniously

Fig. 64 Small pieces of plain and printed, and plain and woven, striped cotton have been pieced with great skill and artistry to make these two hexagon patterns. The simple design of rosettes made with cotton printed in patterned stripes is arranged on a background pieced with plain cotton (see fig. 23). It shows the value of good planning and proportion of pattern to background within a given area. The more complex pattern of hexagons and lozenges is pieced with cotton woven in stripes of varying widths, and plain cotton, in a perfectly balanced, well contrasted arrangement

Fig. 65 Quilted place mat by Ann Mary Pilcher. Hexagon patches of black and white printed cotton have been pieced and applied to the fine linen ground to make this distinctive and well planned design. Notice particularly the ingenious treatment of the corners of the patchwork border, and how the points of the hexagons match the lines of machine stitching to make an attractive pattern of half-hexagons on either side of the border

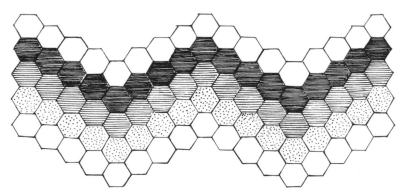

Fig. 66 The Ocean Wave border pattern made with hexagons

and clearly defined. You can easily demonstrate this simple fact for yourself. A second haphazard ring arranged around the first, to make the double rosette, will increase the confusion, and the addition of background patches all of one colour will do little to improve matters. On the other hand, a second carefully selected ring of hexagons in a different colour or tone, when added to the planned rosette, will emphasise the pattern of shape and colour, and well-chosen background patches will further enhance the effect. Enlarging the double rosette with a ring of hexagons of yet another colour or tone will make the treble rosette, and so on. This is one of the earliest known methods of colour planning with the hexagon. (Another pattern and method is mentioned at the end of this section.)

The cushion (fig. 23 and detail fig. 64) and the tea cosy (fig. 30) show two designs made with the single rosette. In each case, the carefully-considered placing and proportion of the pattern in relation to the background area, and to the size and shape of the article, are important factors in the harmony of the final design. Unfortunately, much of the effectiveness of the subtle colour con-trasts in the cushion design are lost in the black and white photograph. In planning a design for a specific purpose, it is a good idea to cut out a pattern of the size and shape of the article in brown paper. If this can be pinned out on a cork mat or other similar surface, the patches can be laid on it and conveniently moved around, like pieces in a jig-saw puzzle, until the final arrangement of colour and pattern is decided. They can then re-main pinned in position until you are ready to seam them, if need be.

Careful preliminary planning of colour and design is especially necessary when working with only one shape, and this begins with the selection of pieces for making the patches. In studying the two examples already mentioned, you will be able to appreciate how much a discerning and disciplined choice (as well as use) of fabrics contributes to the unity of a successful design. The piece-meal nature of patchwork often misleads the inexperienced worker into using too many different colours and too many and varied prints in one piece of work, and once this happens it is difficult to make a coherent and organized design. Until you are exper-ienced in working with shapes and pattern, it is better to limit your choice of colour in some way, perhaps by matching up plain

Fig. 67 Patchwork cushion by Beryl Dean. The six-pointed star motif (made with
the diamond based on the hexagon), is the basis of this rich jewel-like
pattern. It is pieced with consummate skill with fragments of cotton printed
in patterned stripes. Half-diamonds of the cotton print and plain cotton,
in the Dogs tooth pattern, make the surrounding border. The cushion has
a gusset of about one inch in width, pieced with the patterned stripe, and
the edge is finished with a fine piping. The diamond shape, the discerning
and finely balanced use and arrangement of the patterned fabric, and the
subtle contrast of colour and tone all contribute to the success of this superb
design

Fig. 68 The variously patterned star motifs made with the last remnants of the
printed cotton are pieced with plain coloured cotton, to make this more
clearly defined and equally rich mosaic pattern on the back of the cushion.
The well contrasted tone of the plain black and yellow cottons, and the
proportion of pattern to plain background patches, are important elements
in this well balanced and satisfying design

fabrics in one or two colours (or in tones of one colour) with those in a print which particularly appeals to you, or by choosing two colours to predominate, and one other for a background, remembering that the textures and printed designs of the fabrics are further factors lending variety and value to the most limited scheme.

The single rosette and the double rosette can be arranged in a variety of ways to make simple all-over patterns. The illustration in fig. 31 shows a straightforward pattern of double rosettes. A good deal of imaginative thought has been given to the planning of each rosette, both with regard to the colour arrangement and to the use of the cotton prints. The successful assembling of these charming motifs into a well-balanced, richly colourful mosaic pattern is largely due to this preliminary consideration, and to the choice of a sufficiently well-contrasted background colour. All-over patterns of this kind are simple to construct, but disciplined planning of colour, tone, and pattern are essential to good results.

The diamond motif which is developed from the single rosette has been used to make the all-over pattern on the bedcover illustrated in fig. 32. This is a beautifully planned design. The printed cottons of the outer units are of black and white, and yellow and white, each with a ring of hexagons in plain black cotton. Those units within this area are of flowered cotton, black and grey, and a striped cotton print in orange, red and yellow, also with the ring of plain black hexagons which contributes so much to the overall unity of the pattern. The units of the centre area, softer in effect, are alternately a yellow and red print, and a red, grey and turquoise print. The white waffle weave cotton with which the background is pieced gives a rich texture, and a black fringe makes an appropriate finish to this lovely bedcover.

The hexagon can be used to make so many interesting patterns that it is impossible to mention them all. You will easily discover how rosettes can be arranged to make border patterns, but there is one other traditional border pattern which should be mentioned. This is the Ocean Wave (see fig. 66). The wavy line made by the hexagons can be varied according to the arrangement of the coloured and printed patches. This is another method of colour and pattern planning. The Ocean Wave was a popular border pattern for the sides of quilts, but it is not often used today.

In making your own experiments with pattern and colour, do

Fig. 69 Long hexagon shapes of leather applied to a fabric ground and enriched with gold kid and narrow gold cord. This sampler shows an original use of traditional patchwork shapes and might inspire ideas for bags, boxes, belts and other dress accessories in patchwork or patchwork and appliqué. Reproduced by kind permission of the Embroiderers' Guild

Fig. 70 Detail from a patchwork altar frontal by Beryl Dean. Gold lurex fabrics are pieced with silk and velvet patches in a rich mosaic of squares and rectangles. Simple applied shapes and couched metal threads of gold and copper give additional surface enrichment

not be discouraged if your first attempts do not succeed. A great deal can be learned from making mistakes, and you will soon learn from experience what you can do and what you should not do with colour when making patchwork.

Designing with stripes

Ingenuity and resourcefulness in using colour and fabric to make an article which is delightfully decorative and individual, as well as useful, are among the most characteristic gifts of the good patchworker.

The three beautifully designed cushions which are shown on these and the two following pages illustrate an ingenious and imaginative use of fabric and shape to make pattern, which is in the best patchwork tradition.

The very careful exploration of a remnant of cotton fabric printed in even stripes of tones of one colour finally yielded two satisfyingly complete units, each constructed with four triangle shapes. In one, the darkest stripe forms a small square in the centre

Fig. 71 Detail from fig 72. The construction of the patchwork pattern made with this imaginative arrangement of triangles of striped cotton is clearly seen in this photograph

of the unit, with the meeting of the four points of the triangles; in the other, the darkest stripe, arranged along the four outside edges of the unit, outlines a larger square. These two units, which are clearly illustrated in figs 75 and 76, have been combined in the design of the cushion illustrated in fig. 72.

The cushions on these pages show one very personal way of designing with stripes and shapes. Patterns made with woven striped cottons and hexagons can be seen in figs 1 and 64. In studying these, notice the importance of the patches of plain cotton in clarifying the pattern. This is something to remember when you are making your own experiments.

Designing with floral prints

The charming and lively pattern of flowers and leaves made with fragments of printed glazed cotton and small hexagons (fig. 78) shows a different, but equally fascinating way of designing with fabric and shapes. In planning a pattern of this kind it is necessary to select the pieces for each patch with precise care (the window

Fig. 72 One of the three delightful cushions designed by Ann Mary Pilcher to demonstrate different ways of using a striped cotton fabric with a triangle shape to make striking geometric patterns. The alternate arrangement of two separate units, each constructed with four triangles, makes this harmonious and lively pattern

Fig. 73 A design made by the simple repetition of the units made with the small dark square in the centre

Fig. 74 In this design the edges of the units with the darkest stripe on the outside come together to make a strong pattern

Figs 75 and 76 Details showing the construction of the patchwork patterns opposite

Fig. 77 Pincushion by E. M. Gibbons made with small hexagons

template is a great help in doing this), and to arrange them with some regard for the direction of growth. The scale of the flowers and leaves, too, must be right in relation to each other and to the size of the patch. The gay circlet in the illustration, arranged around a centre rosette of plain ivory patches, owes a good deal of its success to this, and to the fact that the background patches have been so carefully considered and well chosen. The cotton of the centre rosette matches the background ivory of the print exactly; the surrounding patches are also ivory coloured but of a slightly different tone, and broken with a faint spot, all of which gives just the right amount of variety to the plain areas without competing with the main design. When planning a design of this kind, it is usually better to confine the colour to the flower sprays or swags and to piece the background all in the same plain fabric, which can be varied in tone or texture to give necessary interest. It is often a good idea to match the background fabric to the background of the print, as in this case.

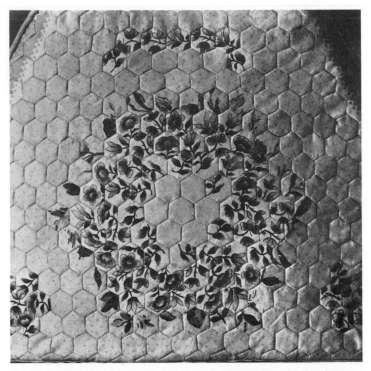

Fig. 78 Detail from a tea cosy by Ronaldine Moorhouse. This charming circlet of flowers and leaves has been most skillfully devized and pieced with fragments of printed glazed cotton in very small hexagons

The Cathedral Window pattern

This is an American pattern, which is made by piecing squares in a most interesting and ingenious manner. The method of working produces an all-over geometrical pattern of stitched fabric which resembles the tracery of a cathedral window, hence its name. The effect is one of the greatest textural richness and delicacy (quite apart from the coloured patches). The construction of this seemingly intricate pattern, which at first glance might appear to be made by quilting, is surprisingly simple and straightforward.

The bedcover illustrated on the following pages (figs 79–81) was made in America about a year ago. The Americans have a splendid tradition and fine inheritance of quilt (and coverlet) making in patchwork and applied work, and this unusual and beautiful bedcover is a worthy successor. The small squares of coloured or printed cottons are bright and fresh against the pure white of the foundation fabric, and although the Cathedral Window does not appear to be a traditional pattern, it would make a handsome furnishing for a bedroom of any period.

Calico has a long tradition of use for patchwork, and is too seldom seen today. Bleached calico is the ideal fabric for making the basic squares for this pattern; it has both crispness and flexibility. It is essential that these are all made of the same white fabric, of course. The coloured pieces are one and three quarter inch squares, cut with the thread of the fabric, and as there is no need for turnings, these can be cut from quite small fragments. Clear, bright colours and small-scale prints look best. As many different colours and prints can be successfully combined in this pattern, it is more effective if the squares are arranged in groups with several plain colours together, and several prints together. If this is taken into consideration when piecing, the squares can be made up in groups, and the placing of each group decided in the final making up.

This pattern has two other very attractive features. The pieced squares automatically make very neat and decorative edges and corners to the bedcover, and a delightful finish to the back of the work. No further lining or finish is required, and the ordered inevitability of this process is most satisfying.

Fig. 79 Detail of the Cathedral Window pattern

Fig. 80 The decorative corner and edge made by the arrangement of the squares

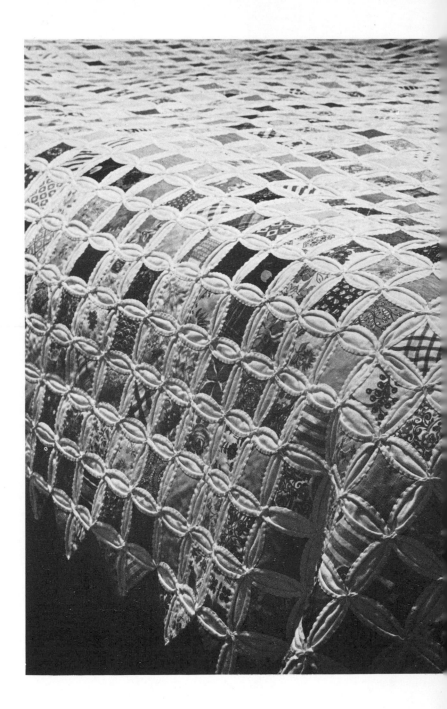

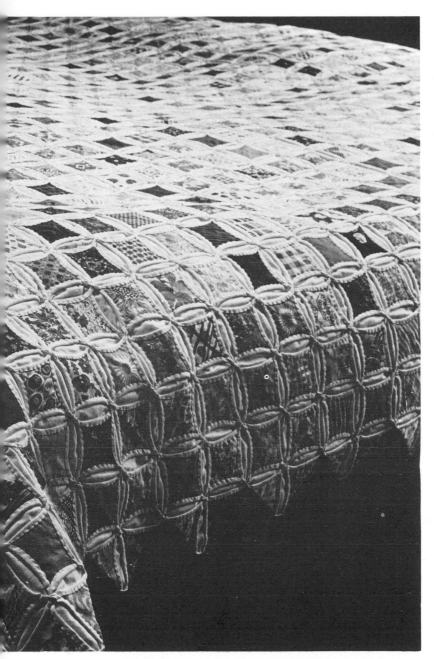

Fig. 81 Bedcover made with the Cathedral Window pattern by Sara Priest. Photographed by kind permission of Elizabeth Hynes

Constructing the patches

The diagrams on the page opposite will help to make the instructions for constructing the patches easy to follow. You will quickly discover the necessity for using a fabric which will fold and crease well in the hand.

1 Cut out a 6-inch square of bleached calico or white poplin with the thread of the fabric. Fold narrow turnings so that the final measurement of the square is $5\,{}^3/_4$ inches (fig. 82A).

2 Fold each corner of the square to the centre, and pin in place as shown (fig. 82B). The square now measures 4 inches.

3 Fold each corner of this square to the centre, and pin in place as before (at the same time removing the first pins). Secure the corners at the centre, two at a time, with a small, firm stitch (fig. 82C). The square now measures $2\,{}^3/_4$ inches.

4 Make a second square, and seam the two together in the usual way.

5 Cut out a $1\,{}^3/_4$-inch square of coloured cotton with the thread of the fabric, and place it over the seamed edge of the two squares as shown in fig. 82D. Pin it carefully in place. Take the folded edge of the white cotton and turn it back over the edge of the coloured cotton, holding it in place between the thumb and first finger of the left hand. Stitch it down with small, even running stitches, which are taken through the coloured cotton and the two thicknesses of the white cotton underneath, to the back of the material (fig. 82F). Two small stitches are taken across the white fabric at each corner to make a firm neat finish (fig. 82E). In the case of a half-square (coming at the edge of an article), the edges of the white and the coloured cottons are turned in and neatly overstitched, as shown on the right-hand side of the diagram.

The pieces of cotton should be carefully pressed before you begin to construct the patches and should not be pressed afterwards, otherwise the distinctive texture is lost. Although this pattern is in many ways similar to a quilting pattern, it is not usually combined with quilting.

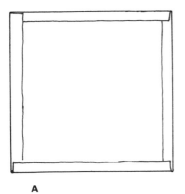

A

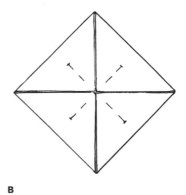

B

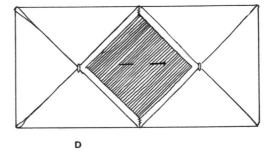

C   **D**

E   **F**

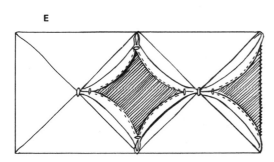

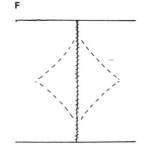

Fig. 82

Patchwork and applied work

It is heartening to know that in both England and America, two countries with a great heritage of beautiful patchwork, there are still dedicated needlewomen who find the time and the desire to make patchwork quilts and bedcovers. The work of two of them is illustrated in this book (figs 32, 81). For a variety of reasons, most needlewomen find a bedcover a more practicable undertaking than a quilt nowadays. Special knowledge, skill and equipment is needed for quilting, and indeed this is a subject on its own which unfortunately cannot be adequately dealt with here. There are other books, mentioned on page 102, in which you will find full information.

Although pieced work is the fundamental patchwork of both countries, quilts and coverlets in applied work are more popular in some country districts of America. One pattern which is popular in both countries, the Garden Basket is shown on page 55. This pattern is made by an arrangement of geometric shapes which have been prepared with a template. The 'blocks', as they are called, are each made separately and applied onto a background material. This pattern depends upon a well planned arrangement of the motifs and well contrasted tone; for this reason the 'blocks' are usually made in one colour – red, green or blue.

The geometric patchwork templates can be used to make a great many motifs which are suitable for applied work. The most obvious one is the hexagon rosette, which can be applied as an all-over pattern or to make a border pattern, with or without other shapes. Stars made with diamonds, and squares can also be used in the same way. The opportunities for pattern making in this way are almost limitless, but great imagination and skill are needed in the planning.

Some of the most delightful applied patterns are made by cutting out flower motifs from a print and composing these into sprays, or alternatively, a complete spray may be cut from the fabric and applied. Yet another method is by cutting out shapes free hand – leaves, birds, fishes, pots or animal shapes – and making an arrangement of these on the background. A lovely example of this kind of appliqué pattern can be seen in a coverlet in the Victoria and Albert Museum. In using either of these methods, the edges of the motif are either turned under and neatly hemmed to the background, (this is called blind appliqué) or, where this is not possible, carefully neatened and sewn with an embroidery stitch such as herringbone, or buttonhole (blanket stitch). In the latter case the shape must be stitched with small tacking stitches about one tenth of an inch from the edge, before working the buttonhole stitch.

Experimenting with applied shapes

It would not be too difficult an exercise for a beginner to arrange a pattern design of hexagon rosettes or diamond star motifs, or squares, to make an applied design for a cushion cover or a cosy, and in doing so, a good deal could be learned about proportion and colour (see page 65). A border for the edge of a short curtain could also be planned with the same motifs, or a decorative bed-head panel, as you became more experienced.

The simple motif illustrated above was made as an experiment by a schoolgirl. It is included as a refreshingly original interpretation of the patchwork-appliqué method. The fish has been developed and enriched with embroidery stitches and sequins from a patchwork shape of squares and triangles, which has been applied to the background. A motif worked out in this way would be delightful for decorating a small object such as a jewel box, or a special belt.

Fig. 83 This motif by Gillian Nievens of the Mary Boon School shows an interesting combination of patchwork, appliqué and embroidery stitches

Fig. 84 Scarecrow by Jennifer MacDowell. One-inch cotton squares have been
pieced with the greatest simplicity to make this lively toy. The hat, too, is
made up with squares

Patchwork toys

Patchwork toys are fun to make, and are engagingly different. They will provide plenty of scope for excercising your originality and ingenuity in a lighthearted way, and once you begin, they tend to develop in all kinds of unexpected ways. The scarecrow on the page opposite (fig. 84) expresses all the gay spontaneity of the happy thought from which he must have taken shape. Florence in her patchwork box (fig. 85) looks appealingly non-plussed, understandably so, for she hides a spring under her check dress and her head is a ping-pong ball. She would delight any child. A hand puppet can provide great opportunities for using

Fig. 85 'Florence' by Margaret Alcock

patchwork in original and inventive ways. The captivating example (fig. 97) has been devized and created with real artistry and imagination, and skilfully made. This is the standard for which you should aim. Kings, princesses, jesters and clowns are popular characters. Among birds and animals the Owl and the Pussycat are good subjects.

Patchwork balls are familiar, and can be made in either of the ways shown in fig. 86, or in sections like an orange. All kinds of other toys can be devized with a little thought and imagination, and you will find that once you begin to work with the fabric and shapes, your ideas will flow.

Small things to make in patchwork

Small things, beautifully made in patchwork, have a special charm and quality. The degree of skill and application which is required in making a small thing perfectly is often considerable, as may be judged from some of the examples in this book, but there is great reward and satisfaction in the achievement.

The assortment of attractive articles illustrated on these pages give the delightful impression of having been left behind on the sea shore. Each one is a highly individual piece of work, yet the shape and construction of each is simple. It is the imaginative use of fabric and geometric shape which gives to each its particular character.

The pincushion on the right, in fig. 87, has been pieced with fragments of genuine Victorian cotton. It is made by joining two hexagon rosettes. The star-shaped pin cushion on the left is made with six pentagonal shapes arranged round a centre hexagon. A beginner could enjoy working with either of these patterns to make an individual pincushion with materials of her own choice.

The skill entailed in constructing and making the exquisite

Fig. 86 An unusual pincushion made with hexagons; and two balls, one made with hexagons and squares, the other with pentagons, by Ann Mary Pilcher

Fig. 87 Three pincushions, the centre one by Patricia Horne, the two smaller ones by Miriam Moore

Fig. 88 Patchwork workbox by Doris Cook

Fig. 89 Patchwork box by Ann Mary Pilcher

pincushions in fig. 44 is very probably beyond most of us. It is hardly possible to credit that these difficult shapes, the half long diamond and the diamond, could have been pieced with such perfect precision from small scraps of Lurex fabrics. The diamond construction which is the smaller of the two would fit into a cube shaped box of about two and a half inch measurement.

A small trinket box, made in silk patchwork and quilted inside can be a lovely thing to make and to possess. In making a box of any size it is usually better to construct it yourself from good card than to try to cover a ready-made box; this can lead to all kinds of difficulties, and, in trying to fit the box, the patchwork may be spoiled.

Two examples of well designed and well made boxes can be seen in figs 13, 88. The work box, and the needle case and other articles in fig. 90 belong together. They are pieced in $\frac{3}{4}$-inch squares in plain and printed cottons. The discerning choice and use of the fabrics (the box is lined with the print), suggests that this is the work of an experienced and knowledgeable patch-worker. It is, in fact, a practised needlewoman's first successfully finished patchwork (after an unsuccessful attempt).

There are no short cuts in learning any craft, and skill and experience will only be gained through patient practice in working with the materials and methods, and by trial and error. This will not be irksome if your whole interest is engaged, and in making small things as well as you can, you will be learning a great deal in a most enjoyable way. If your work is thorough at every stage your progress will be sound and sure, and you will save yourself much disappointment and frustration. The ability and knowledge you acquire in making the small things can all be applied to the larger things in due course.

Fig. 90 The needlecase, thimble container and scissors case which belong to the workbox by Doris Cook in fig. 88

Fig. 91

Patchwork in relation to dress and accessories

It is interesting to observe how thoroughly the present revival of interest in patchwork, or the idea of patchwork, has permeated our lives, and to discover the extraordinarily diverse forms it takes. Plastic shopping bags, gift wrapping paper, cotton, and nylon fur-fabric are all to be found printed in traditional patchwork patterns. Tote bags, leather jerkins and waistcoats, trouser suits and expensive leather handbags are all to be seen made in patchwork. Some of this work is very good, much is mediocre, and some nasty. The interesting fact which emerges most clearly however is that of all the geometric shapes, it is the square, with its component the triangle, which is usually the most satisfying and successful, whether printed on a cheap plastic shopping bag or fashioned with fine leather to make a good handbag.

The sketches in fig. 91 were made with this in mind, for it seems that this most basic of shapes is the one with which we may hope to work successfully in a modern idiom (which is essential in matters of dress). It could well be in the field of dress and dress accessories that the serious patchworker will find some of the greatest opportunities for developing ideas, and for cont-

Fig. 92 A detail from the panel in fig. 93, which might suggest ways in which padding embroidery stitches, or metal threads, could be combined with patchwork for dress purposes and accessories

Fig. 93 A panel by Janet Speak which shows a flexible and imaginative approach
to patchwork. Fabrics (which include printed cotton, gingham, and corduroy velvet) and shapes have been carefully selected and skilfully arranged
to create a rich and well integrated pattern. Padding, metal threads, and
embroidery stitches provide additional surface enrichment and textural
interest

tributing something towards the development of the true character of patchwork.

Leather is a commodity which is as universally used as woven fabric nowadays, and off-cuts of coloured leather are almost as easy to obtain as pieces of coloured fabric. Experiments might be made in piecing leather, or cutting out shapes to apply. Belts offer great possibilities for patchwork in leather or fabric. Coloured suedes, with the introduction of a little gold kid, can make rich and lovely items — bags, slippers and boxes, as well as belts. Leather can be cut and seamed edge to edge in the same way as fabric patches (but no papers are needed of course). The stitches should not be too close together, and the tension must allow flexibility. A very fine needle should be used, and if you take it twice into each stitch, you will be using a gloving stitch, which is very suitable. A fine gloving thread would be the ideal thread.

Patchwork in fabric can be combined with padding, which is another popular feature at the present time. In this case the object would be to provide enrichment, rather than warmth. Pockets, bands, borders, yokes — the possibilities of all these might be explored — and with shapes other than the square of course.

Fig. 94 shows a very good example of what is called crazy patchwork. This method uses irregular-shaped pieces, which are tacked and finally sewn to a ground material. A considerable degree of skill is required if the work is to be as disciplined and accomplished as this example. It is all too easy to get the worst kind of crazy-paving effect. This method of patchwork was popular in Victorian times, but is not often used today. The shapes in this kimono have each been sewn with feather stitching, which is the traditional method. This feather stitching is done in the hand, after the shapes have been arranged and tacked in position on the ground fabric.

Fig. 94 Kimono in crazy patchwork by A. P. Mitchell

Finishing and lining

The sewing in of the final patch, successfully completing a piece of work which has demanded hours of patient application, will bring a feeling of satisfaction and achievement. No matter what the frustrations and difficulties encountered and overcome in the process, it will all seem worthwhile for this one moment of reward, and the sight of the completed work spread out before you.

Many people find the task of finishing and lining which still lies ahead much less delightful. The importance of this being done with as much care and consideration as the construction of the patchwork cannot be overemphasized. A beautifully pieced article can be completely ruined by insufficient time and care being spent on the finishing and making up. Similarly a less perfect piece can be enhanced by meticulous care at this stage.

If the work has been properly handled and kept during the making, the task will be much more straightforward and the finished result will be fresher and crisper.

Pressing and removing the papers

The papers must be removed from all articles which will require laundering. Spread the work out on a flat surface, and snip the tackings (basting stitches), removing the odd threads without disturbing the papers. It is now that you will appreciate the absence of knots and back stitches. The work should be pressed firmly and evenly (on the wrong side) before the papers are removed. Remove the papers carefully, after pressing, so that the work is disturbed as little as possible. Undamaged papers can be saved for future use.

At this stage the edges will require straightening, or neatening, and where half patches have been sewn in, it may help to tack the turnings lightly to keep the edge firm.

Edge finishes

Edge finishes will be chosen for their suitability for the particular patchwork article and should always be as plain and simple as possible. The finish of all the articles in this book is so good that it has probably not intruded on your attention. Now is the time to study them.

There is no reason why cushion covers or other articles with straight edges should not be seamed on the sewing machine if this is suitable. Sometimes a decorative edge will be made automatically by the arrangement of the shapes, and this is very satisfactory.

A piping always makes a good looking edge, and is well worth the little extra time spent in preparation and stitching. A piping is made with strips of material, cut on the bias, to the required width. The strip is folded and pressed before tacking and slip stitching in place. The colour should match the background or pick up one of the colours in the work. The same method is used for piping with a cord.

The traditional way of finishing off the edges of a bedcover is the most straightforward. The edges of the patchwork and the lining are folded in and stitched together with small even running stitches, one row just below the fold, and the second about a quarter of an inch away.

Linings

Linings are necessary for neatening and protecting the back of the patchwork, and to preserve the shape in wear. The lining material should be firm, and appropriate in weight and colour to the patchwork it is to line. It should always be cut on the straight.

It is usually not essential to line a cushion cover, but cosies require lining, and delicate materials will wear longer if lined.

Interlinings are sometimes needed for warmth. Carded wool, Domette (medium to heavyweight white flannel) and Terylene (Dacron) wadding are all good for this purpose, or more economically, pieces of used blanket are excellent.

Fig. 95

Pads and fillings

It is more practical to make pads for cushions and tea cosies, so that the covers can easily be removed for laundering. A cushion pad should always be made a little larger than the cover it is going to fill. Make sure that it is stuffed evenly and well, and that the corners are well filled.

Sheeps' wool is the ideal filling for most purposes, if it can be obtained, but Kapok and Terylene (polyester, such as Dacron) down are good. Blanket or flannel, cut to shape, can be used for tea cosies, or Domette (flannel) and Kapok are suitable. Bran is still occasionally used for pincushions, but sheeps' wool and Kapok are more pleasant and easier to use.

Foam rubber pads are excellent as filling for chair cushions, or any cushion which has a gusset. For balls, sheeps' wool is best (it washes well and retains the shape), but Kapok or foam rubber

Fig. 96 Three examples of well made and well finished patchwork. Book cover by K. Barlow, blotter and stamp book by E. N. Lawson, and workbox by Alison Timmins

filling are suitable alternatives. Kapok or sheeps' wool are good for stuffing toys, but foam filling is not very good for this purpose.

Fastenings

Fastenings, especially on boxes and bags, can easily spoil the whole thing if they are not just right. The scale of the fastening is as important as the manner of it. The addition of something extraneous seems particularly noticeable with patchwork, and it is essential that it should be unobtrusive. An example of a fastening which is perfectly a part of the whole article can be seen in fig. 11. The two boxes illustrated in figs 13, 88 have solved the problem with well-fitting covers, and no fastenings. The knobs for lifting off have been designed as part of the whole. Buttons, unless hand-made, and beads particularly, should be avoided. The genuine patchwork button, which is made with two small hexagons, is charming, and would hardly ever be out of place. It is made by stuffing two small hexagons sewn together, with a shank left for attaching the button to the article.

In conclusion

Many people have been inspired to learn the craft of patchwork as a result of seeing a lovely piece by chance – in a friend's house, in an exhibition – or by hearing a talk about it. Most thrifty needle-women have cherished pieces saved up, waiting to be made into something beautiful and special one day. But unless there is some-one at hand to give help and guidance, it can be difficult to know how and where to begin.

The aim of this book has been threefold. In the first place, to introduce the traditional patchwork shapes and methods of working, and to give you practical help in using them; secondly, to show with good examples how these can be used with contem-porary fabrics in a variety of imaginative and attractive ways, and thirdly, to encourage you to experiment boldly with shapes and fabrics of your own choice.

It is the disciplined and inventive use of the fabrics within a well planned framework, which gives to early patchwork its unique character and charm. These are the qualities for which you should aim in your own work. This is not a recommendation to copy the work of the past (unless the very best examples, for purposes of study). Far from it, it is saying that if your own is to be as full of life and character as the best examples of the past, it must be created in the spirit of the present time, taking into account the different ways of being inventive with contemporary fabrics, and the different reasons and purposes, and places, for which your patchwork will be made.

There is much more enjoyment to be gained from working out your own ideas and patterns, and so long as you do not attempt too much, too soon, there is no reason why you should not achieve some satisfying and delightful results. The early patchworkers were not trained artist craftsmen, yet they made magnificent works of art, and you should not be afraid to be adventurous in your ideas and your plans. You will not discover your full potent-ialities until you begin to use them.

Fig. 97 This enchanting hand puppet shows a well thought out and discerning use of fabric and shapes to make a distinctive design. The plain patches have been carefully related to the printed fabric, in colour and tone, so that the overall effect is balanced and harmonious. The tassels and rings add gaiety and a touch of contrasting colour, and the hair is made with closely sewn black bugle beads. Reproduced by kind permission of the Embroiderers' Guild

For further reading

Patchwork by Averil Colby; Batsford, London 1958; Branford, Newton Centre, Mass.

Patchwork quilts by Averil Colby; Batsford, London 1965; Scribner, New York 1966

Old Patchwork quilts by Ruth E. Finley; Grosset and Dunlop, New York 1929; Branford, Newton Centre, Mass. 1970

Patchwork today by Doris E. Marston; Bell, London 1968; Branford, Newton Centre, Mass.

Introducing patchwork by Alice Timmins; Batsford, London 1968; Watson-Guptill, New York 1968

Fun with appliqué and patchwork by Ilse Strobl-Wohlschlager; Batsford, London 1970; Watson-Guptill, New York 1970

Quilts and coverlets by Jean Ray Laury; Van Nostrand-Reinhold, New York 1970

List of suppliers

Quilt patterns (mail order): Aunt Martha's Studios, 1245 Swift Avenue, Kansas City, Missouri 64116. Sterns and Foster Co., Cincinnati, Ohio 45215. Mrs Danner's Quilts, Box 650, Emporia, Kansas 66801

Patchwork kits (mail order): Bernard Ulman Co., 2030 Thomson Avenue, Long Island City, New York. Paragon Needlecraft, 367 Southern Boulevard, Bronx, New York

General equipment (mail order): Leewards, Elgin, Illinois 60120. Herrscher's, Hoover Road, Steven's Point, Wisconsin 55481. Marribee, 2904 West Lancaster Street, Fort Worth, Texas 76107

Acknowledgements

The author would like to express her thanks to all those people whose work appears in this book. Also to the Provost of King's College, Cambridge for permission to reproduce a detail from the altar frontal in the college chapel, fig. 62; to Miss Constance Howard and Goldsmiths' College School of Art for permission to photograph and reproduce a student's work, fig. 93; to Mrs Elizabeth Hynes for allowing her American bedcover to be photographed and included, fig. 81; to the Embroiderers' Guild for the photograph of the hand puppet from their collection, fig. 97; and to the Victoria and Albert Museum for figs 4, 5, 6 and 7.

With the exception of these five last mentioned, and figs 2, 3, 62, 94 and 96, all the photographs are by John Gay, to whom special thanks are due, as also to Miss Phyllis Gibbon who typed the manuscript.

Index

Set in 9 point Univers
Printed and bound by Parish Press, Inc.